AF647735

hindi
KAY BOL

India - a Celebration
भारत एक पर्व

Priya Gupta

Swapnil Kapoor

Designed by 'www.arcreativewings.com'

ISBN Paperback: 978-93-5906-661-5
ISBN Hardcover: 978-93-5813-716-3
Library of Congress Control Number: 2023911134

First Edition 2023
Printed in China

Published by Hindi Kay Bol
Connecticut, USA
www.hindikaybol.com
Follow us on FB / IG @ hindikaybol

For more resources related to this book, including an audio file of all Hindi poems, scan the QR code below:

Among different religions and cultures, India celebrates more than 50 festivals in a year. These festivals form an integral part of the rich heritage of the country, along with the languages spoken around the land.

The "why" and "how" of each festival is important, but what holds more value in the globalized world, is an appreciation of the spirit behind each festival. I have written this book to reflect the fervor and happiness behind each celebration. I hope that young minds resonate with these thoughts and learn to develop a tolerance for every culture at an early age.

कर सूर्य को नमन
होता संक्रांति का आगमन,
रेवड़ी, गज्जक, खिचड़ी, तिल
खाएँ मिलकर सब जन।

कहीं पतंगो का पर्व,
कहीं सेवा और दान,
त्योहार एक नाम अनेक
माघी, पोंगल, उत्तरायन।

People bow to the Sun and pray,
as *Makar Sankranti* brings the first golden ray.
Feast begins on the winter spread
made of peanuts and sesame.

Kites soar in the sky,
offerings flow in donation.
In different names, the festival unites,
Maghi, Pongal, Uttarayan.

होली

उड़ा गुलाल, उड़ा गुलाल,
हरा, नीला, पीला, लाल,
पिचकारी में पानी भर कर
खेलें हम सुबह से शाम।

टेसू के फूल लाल
मिला पानी, हुआ धमाल,
आज नहाना होगा जम कर
होली के हैं रंग कमाल।

Colors fly in the sky,
green, blue, yellow and red.
From dawn to dusk, kids play
with water guns, laughing away.

Bright red blooms the *Tesu* flower
a riot of color when mixed in water,
today is the day for a good scrub
as *Holi* colors paint and rub.

आयी फसल की बहार,
लायी बैसाखी का त्योहार।
सुनो सुनहरा खेत बुलाए,
भँगड़ा करने आए यार।

खाया सबने सरसों का साग,
मक्की की रोटी के साथ,
खुशी में सब झूमें नाचे,
डाले हाथों में हाथ।

The bounty of winter harvest
brings along *Baisakhi*,
the golden fields beckon
the friends ready for *Bhangra* beat.

They savor *Sarson ka saag*
accompanied by *Makki ki roti*.
All dance, celebrating abundance,
with cheer and glee.

रोज़े हुए पूरे आज
बाज़ारों में दिखता साज,
चाँद-रात का जश्न है
'ईद मुबारक' आई आवाज़।

शुरू हुई खरीदारी
हीना से सजे हाथ,
बच्चों, कल मिलेगी ईदी
बिरयानी और सेवइयाँ साथ।

Today marks the fast's completion,
bazaars are alive with festive decorations.
Under the new moon's radiant glow,
"Eid Mubarak" echoes, sweet salutations flow.

Tonight, the shopping commences,
women's hands adorned with intricate henna.
Tomorrow, the young ones shall receive their Eidi,
amidst fragrant biryani and sevaiyaan.

राखी की डोरी में बंधी
बचपन की हर लड़ाई,
शिकायत का पिटारा,
आँख-मिचौली, छिपन-छिपाई।

जब लाँघ लिया बचपन,
डोरी बनी रक्षा का बंधन,
यही भाई बहन का प्यार,
दर्शाता राखी का त्योहार।

Within the *Rakhi's* sacred tie,
lie bittersweet memories of fights gone by.
The box of complaints, once held tight;
games of hide-n-seek and I spy.

When it reaches adulthood
the *Rakhi* turns into a promise of protection.
This bond between siblings
is the essence of *Raksha bandhan*.

स्वतंत्रता दिवस

जब स्वतंत्र आकाश में
उड़ते पंछी और पतंग,
तिरंगा भी खूब लहराए
हर झोंके के संग।

सोच की आज़ादी से
होता पूरा देश सम्पन्न,
15 अगस्त का संदेश है
भाईचारा और अमन।

When birds and kites fly,
in the open sky.
And the Tricolor flutters high,
with every hint of breeze.

Through the freedom of thought,
the nation achieves true independence.
The message of 15th August is clear,
to foster brotherhood and peace.

पूकलम की सुगंध से
महका पूरा केरल,
आयोजित है नौका दौड़
पकी धान की फसल।

सद्या खाएँ बच्चे - बूढ़े
भर केले के पत्तल,
महाबली आए देखने घर
अपनी प्रजा समृद्ध और सफल।

Onam

Kerala exudes a scent divine,
Pookalam is set in floral design.
Snake boats race with all the might,
rice crops ripe, harvest's golden light.

A feast of nine courses on banana leaf,
served to all, a culinary treat.
Mahabali, the King, his realm he visits,
to witness his people celebrate.

मैया ने रखा उपवास,
पापा ने बनाया प्रसाद,
मीरा आज सजी कृष्णा-सी,
है मधुर हाथ में बंसी।

जन्माष्टमी के गीत पुराने
कहते लीला कृष्ण की,
मंदिर और मेले लगे लुभावने,
जैसे माखन में मिश्री।

Today, mom observes a sacred fast,
while dad prepares *Prasad.*
The little one is dressed as *Krishna*
with a flute in her hands, a divine aura.

Ancient songs of *Janmashtami* resound,
narrating Krishna's birth, stories abound.
Temples and fairs, a captivating sight,
like butter mixed with *Mishri,* pure delight.

नवरात्रि

उत्तर में कन्या पूजन,
गुजरात में रास-गरबा,
दक्षिण में गोलू सजा,
संग सरस्वती पूजा।

हर राज्य में अलग
नौ रातों की जगमग,
देवी शक्ति का उत्सव
नवरात्रि का पावन पर्व।

The festival of *Navratri*,
is a celebration of the female divine might.
In ways unique to its place of origin,
but essentially, a festivity of nine nights.

As *Kanya Poojan* in the North,
Raas Garba in Gujarat.
Golu in the south of India,
and *Saraswati Pooja*.

दशहरा

कुल्लू से मैसूर तक
मनाए भारत दशहरा,
उत्तर में रावण-दहन
पूरब में दुर्गा पूजा।

मेले, झांकी, और लोक गीत
दिखें जगह-जगह सभी,
बुराई पर अच्छाई की जीत
यही है विजय दशमी की रीत।

Across India, *Dussehra* unfolds its stage,
from *Kullu* to *Mysore*, in different shades.
In the North, *Ravana's* effigies blaze,
while the East is immersed in *Durga's* grace.

Fairs, processions and folk songs
fill the air with vibrance.
At the heart, the triumph of good prevails,
Vijay Dashmi's tradition, where evil fails.

चौखट पर तोरण लटकायी
हमने नई रंगोली बनायी,
अमावस की रात लायी
घर-घर दीपक और मिठाई ।

अंतर मन से मिटे अंधेरा
तब उज्जवल हो संसार,
लक्ष्मी का वास वहाँ
होता जहाँ स्नेह और प्यार ।

In the doorway, a *toran* is hung,
and the floor is adorned with *Rangoli*.
The home is lit up with *diyas*,
as the new moon brings *Diwali*.

As darkness flees the heart and mind,
the world becomes a place brighter.
Lakshmi comes to reside,
in a dwelling of love and care.

गुरु नानक ने सिखलाई
जन सेवा और भक्ति,
पूरी दुनिया को दिखलायी
कथा-कीर्तन की शक्ति।

लगा है आज लंगर
सजा है गुरुद्वारा,
जन्मदिन गुरु नानक का
गुरु पूरब कहलाता।

Guru Nanak enlightened the world,
on the path of service and devotion.
He untapped the power within,
through worship and *keertan*.

Today, the *Gurudwara* is lit up,
and there's *Langar* for all.
The birthday of Guru Nanak,
is celebrated as *Guru Purab*.

आँखे मीचे सोये बच्चे
कुछ हलचल सुनी सपने में,
शायद उतरा स्लेड छत पे
या फिर संता चिम्नी से।

सुबह दिखा उपहार का ढेर
जहाँ था क्रिसमस का पेड़,
सपरिवार खाना खाया
सबने मिल आभार जताया।

Children slumbered, tucked in with care,
footsteps whispered through winter air.
Was it a sleigh's touch or Santa's grand glide,
down the chimney, secrets to hide?

In the morning, a heap of gifts they found,
where the Christmas tree was.
And ate together with their kin,
with gratitude in their hearts.

More festivals of India

Bihu [be-hoo] - Bihu is a set of three important cultural festivals unique to the Indian state of Assam– 'Rongali' or 'Bohag Bihu' observed in April, 'Kati Bihu' observed in October or November, and 'Bhogali' observed in January. The Rongali Bihu celebrates the arrival of spring. Kati Bihu marks the replanting of rice saplings, and Bhogali Bihu marks the end of the harvesting season.

Lohri [loh-re] - Lohri is a popular winter Punjabi folk festival celebrated primarily in Northern India. Lohri marks the end of winter and a traditional welcome of longer days. It is celebrated with a bonfire in small gatherings.

Pongal [pohn-gull] - Pongal is the harvest festival of the people of the state of Tamil Nadu, celebrated in mid-January. The four-day festival honors the Sun God. The four days of the Pongal festival are called Bhogi Pongal, Surya / Thai Pongal, and Mattu Pongal, Kaanum Pongal. Pongal is also the name of a sweetened dish of rice boiled in milk and jaggery that is ritually consumed on this festival.

Republic Day - Republic Day is when India celebrates the day on which the Constitution of India came into effect on 26 January 1950. A celebration is held in the national capital, New Delhi, at the Rajpath before the President of India. On this day, ceremonious parades take place, which are performed as a tribute to India; its unity in diversity, and its rich cultural heritage.

Maha Shivratri [mah-She-v-raat-re] - Literally meaning "The Great Night of Shiva" is a Hindu festival celebrated annually in honor of the deity Shiva. The festival commemorates the wedding of Shiva and Parvati and the occasion that Shiva performs his divine dance, called the Tandava.

Ram Navami [raam-now-me] - A Hindu festival that celebrates the birth of Rama, one the most popularly revered deities in Hinduism, also known as the seventh avatar of Vishnu. He is often held as an emblem within Hinduism for being an ideal king and human through his righteousness, good conduct, and virtue.

Mahavir Jayanti [mah-veer-juh-yun-tee] - Mahavir Jayanti is the most important religious festival for Jains. It marks the birth of Mahavira, the last of Jain saints and religious gurus.

Navroz [nuv-roz] – Navroz is the Parsi New Year. On this day, Parsis clean the house and decorate it with flowers and rangoli to make it look beautiful and welcoming for visitors. Dressed up in traditional attire, they visit the Fire Temple after breakfast and perform a prayer called Jashan to express gratitude to the Lord, pray for prosperity, and seek His forgiveness.

Buddha Purnima [buddha-poor-nima]- Buddha Purnima is a Buddhist festival that is celebrated in many parts of Asia, commemorating the birth of the prince Siddhartha Gautama, who became the Gautama Buddha and founded Buddhism.

Rath Yatra [ruth-yaat-ra] - The term particularly refers to the annual Ratha Yatra in Odisha, Jharkhand, West Bengal and other East Indian states, particularly the Odia festival that involve a public procession with a chariot with deities Jagannath (Vishnu avatar), Balabhadra (his brother), Subhadra (his sister) and Sudarshana Chakra (his weapon) on a ratha, a wooden deula-shaped chariot.

Gandhi Jayanti [Gandhi-juh-yun-tee] - Gandhi Jayanti is an event celebrated to mark the birthday of Mahatma Gandhi. It is celebrated annually on 2 October, and is one of the three national holidays of India. The UN General Assembly announced on 15 June 2007 that it adopted a resolution which declared that 2 October will be celebrated as the International Day of Non-Violence in honor of Gandhi.

Ganesh Chaturthi [gun-esh-cha-toor-thee]- Ganesh Chaturthi is a Hindu festival commemorating the birth of the Hindu god Ganesha. The festival is marked with the installation of Ganesha's clay idols privately in homes and publicly on elaborate pandals (temporary stages).

Chhath Puja [chuthh-pooja]- Chhath is an ancient Hindu festival historically native to the Indian subcontinent, more specifically, the Indian states of Bihar, Uttar Pradesh, Jharkhand, and the Nepalese provinces of Madhesh and Lumbini. Prayers during Chhath puja are dedicated to the solar deity, Surya, to show gratitude and thankfulness for bestowing the bounties of life on earth and to request that certain wishes be granted.

Glossary

Baisakhi [bae-saa-khi] - The festival of wheat harvest primarily celebrated in North India.

Bhangra [bhaang-ra] - A type of high-energy traditional folk dance of Punjab area.

Biryani [bir-ya-nee] - A mixed rice dish with ancient origins in South Asia. It is made with spices, vegetables, rice, and usually some type of meat.

Diwali [dee-wa-lee] - Celebrated as the day Rama returned to his kingdom in Ayodhya with his wife Sita and his brother Lakshmana after defeating the demon king Ravana. The festival is an annual homecoming and bonding period not only for families, but also for communities and associations.

Diya [dee-ya] - An earthen lamp made from clay or mud with a cotton wick dipped in oil or ghee.

Durga [door-ga] - Literally meaning invincible, Durga is a Hindu goddess, worshipped in many forms. She is associated with protection, strength, motherhood, destruction, and wars. Durga's legend centers around combating evils and demonic forces that threaten peace, prosperity, and dharma, representing the power of good over evil.

Dusshera [duss-hera] - Dussehra is a Sanskrit compound word composed of daśama 'tenth' and ahar 'day', connoting the festival on the tenth day celebrating the victory of good over evil.

Eid Mubarak [eid-mouba-ruk] - Meaning "blessed festival", Muslims all over the world use it as a greeting on the feast as a cultural tradition.

Eidi [e-dee] - A tradition where the older generation provides monetary gifts to the younger generation in their family and community on the festival of Eid.

Golu [go-loo] - The festive display of dolls and figurines in South India during the autumn festive season, particularly around the multiday Navaratri. They are also known Gombe Habba, Bommai golu, or Bommala Koluvu.

Guru Nanak [guru-naan-uk] - Guru Nanak was the founder of Sikhism and is the first of the ten Sikh Gurus. His birth is celebrated worldwide as Gurupurab.

Gurudwara [guru-dwar-aa] - Literal meaning "Door to the Guru", Gurudwara is a place of assembly and worship for Sikhs. Sikhs also refer to gurudwaras as Gurdwara Sahib. People from all faiths are welcomed in gurdwaras.

Holi [ho-lee] - Holi is a popular and significant Hindu festival celebrated worldwide as the Festival of Colors, love and spring. It celebrates the eternal and divine love of the gods Radha and Krishna.

Janmashtmi [jun-maash-tummy] - Janmashtmi is an annual Hindu festival that celebrates the birth of Krishna, the eighth avatar of Vishnu. The celebratory customs associated with Janmashtami include a celebration festival, reading and recitation of religious texts, dance and enactments of the life of Krishna.

Kanya Poojan [kun-ya poo-jun] - A Hindu holy ritual, the Kanya Poojan ceremony primarily involves the worship of nine girls, representing the nine forms of Goddess Durga (Navdurga). As per Hindu philosophy, these girls are considered as the manifestation of the natural force of creation.

Keertan [keer-tun] - Keertan is a Sanskrit word that means "narrating, reciting, telling, describing" of an idea or story, specifically in Indian religions. It also refers to a genre of religious performance arts, connoting a musical form of narration or shared recitation, particularly of spiritual or religious ideas.

Kerala [kar-ella] is a state on India's tropical Malabar Coast, known for its palm-lined beaches and backwaters, a network of canals. Inland are the Western Ghats, mountains whose slopes support tea, coffee and spice plantations as well as wildlife.

Krishna [krish-na] - Krishna is a major deity in Hinduism. He is worshipped as the eighth avatar of Vishnu and also as the Supreme God in his own right. He is a central character in the Mahabharata, the Bhagavata Purana, the Brahma Vaivarta Purana, and the Bhagavad Gita, and is mentioned in many Hindu philosophical, theological, and mythological texts.

Kullu [kool-u] - Kullu is a town in the Indian state of Himachal Pradesh, known for its temples and hills covered with pine and Himalayan cedar forests and sprawling apple orchards. Historical references about the Kullu valley dates to ancient Hindu literary works of Ramayana, Mahabharata and the Puranas.

Lakshmi [luck-shmee] - Lakshmi is one of the principal goddesses in Hinduism. She is the goddess of wealth, fortune, power, beauty, fertility and prosperity.

Langar [lung-urh] - Langar is the community kitchen of a gurdwara, which serves meals to all free of charge, regardless of religion, caste, gender, economic status, or ethnicity. People sit on the floor and eat together, and the kitchen is maintained and serviced by Sikh community volunteers who are doing seva or "selfless services."

Maghi [maag-hee] - A different name used for the festival of Makar Sakranti, in the Indian states of Himachal and Jammu and some regions of Punjab.

Mahabali [mah-bulee] - In ancient Kerala, King Mahabali was the noblest and most prosperous ruler, who transformed his kingdom into a heavenly place. His legend is a major part of the annual festival Onam.

Makki ki roti [mukky-ki-roh-tee]- Makki ki roti is a flat unleavened bread made from corn meal (maize flour), primarily eaten in North India and also in Nepal. Like most rotis in the Indian subcontinent, it is baked on a tava.

Mishri [mih-sh-re] - Misri refers to crystallized sugar lumps, and a type of confectionery mineral, which has its origins in India and Iran, also known as rock sugar, elsewhere. In Hinduism, mishri may be offered to a deity as offering and distributed as prasad. God Krishna is said to be fond of makkhan (butter) and misri.

Mysore [my-sore] - Mysore, officially Mysuru, is a metropolitan city in the southern Indian state of Karnataka. Known for its heritage structures and palaces, including the famous Mysore Palace, and noted for its culture, Mysore is popularly known as the "City of Palaces", the "Heritage City". During the Dusshera festivals, Mysore receives hundreds of thousands of tourists from around the world.

Navratri [nuv-raat-re]- Navratri (Sanskrit for nine nights) is an annual Hindu festival observed in the honor of the Goddess, in various forms.

Pongal [pohn-gul]- Pongal is a multi-day Hindu harvest festival celebrated by Tamils in India. According to tradition, the festival marks the end of winter solstice, and the start of the sun's six-month-long journey northwards when the sun enters the Capricorn, also called as Uttarayana. The festival is named after the ceremonial "Pongal", which means "to boil, overflow" and refers to the traditional dish prepared from the new harvest of rice boiled in milk with jaggery.

Pookalam [pook-a-luhm] - The floral Rangoli, known as Pookalam, is made out of the gathered blossoms with several varieties of flowers of differing tints pinched up into little pieces to design and decorate patterns on the floor, particularly at entrances and temple premises like a flower mat. Lamps are arranged in the middle or edges.

Prasad [pra-saadh] - Prasadam or Prasad is a religious offering in Hinduism. Most often Prasad is vegetarian food offered to devotees after thanksgiving to God.

Raas Garba [raas-gur-baa] - Garba is a form of dance which originates from the state of Gujarat in India. The name is derived from the Sanskrit term Garbh (womb). Many traditional garbas are performed around a centrally lit lamp or a picture or statue of the Goddess Shakti.

Raavan [raa-wuhn] - The multi-headed rakshasa (demon) king of the island of Lanka, and the chief antagonist in the Hindu epic Ramayana.

Rakhi [raak-hee] - Sisters of all ages tie an amulet called the Rakhi around the wrists of their brothers, on the festival of Raksha Bandhan.

Rangoli [rung-oly] - Rangoli is an art form that originates from India, in which patterns are created on the floor or a tabletop using materials such as powdered limestone, red ochre, dry rice flour, colored sand, quartz powder, flower petals, and colored rocks.

Sankranti [sunk-raan-tee] - Sankranti refers to the transmigration of the sun from one zodiac to another in Indian astronomy.

Saraswati [sir-us-vutee]- Saraswati is the Hindu goddess of knowledge, music, art, speech, wisdom, and learning. She is generally shown to have four arms, holding a book, a rosary, a water pot, and a musical instrument called the veena.

Sarson ka Saag [Sir-so-ka-saag]- A dish of mustard greens cooked with spices. It originated in the north of the Indian subcontinent and is popular throughout the region.

Sevaiyaan [save-ayi-yaa] - A pudding style dessert made out of vermicelli, milk, sugar and cardamom, popularly on Eid.

Tesu [tay-soo] – A fiery red flower of a tree commonly referred to as flame-of-the-forest, dhak, palash, and bastard teak. Revered as sacred by Hindus, it is prized for producing an abundance of vivid blooms, and is used to prepare a traditional Holi colour called "Kesari".

Toran [towr-uh-nuh] - Torana is a sacred or honorific gateway in Buddhist and Hindu architecture, often freestanding and sometimes ornamental on festivals, hung in a doorway.

Uttarayan [utther-aa-yun] - The Uttarayan is derived from two different Sanskrit words – "uttara" (North) and "ayana" (movement), thus indicating the northward movement of the Sun, another name for Sankranti.

Vijaydashmi [vee-jay-dush-me]- is a compound of the two words vijaya 'victory' and daśamī 'tenth', connoting the festival on the tenth day celebrating the victory of good over evil.

Priya Gupta is the founder and author at Hindi Kay Bol publishing. She founded Hindi Kay Bol with a vision to make bilingual books accessible to kids worldwide, and help multicultural families keep the language tradition alive. She lives in Connecticut, US with her husband and two kids and draws her inspiration to write from nature, Indian arts and culture, and her family.

Swapnil Kapoor is a passionate illustrator born in India and now living in England. Swapnil discovered her artistic abilities at an early age and nurtured them alongside her pursuit of a career in automotive engineering. When not bringing illustrations to life, she spends her time running after her toddler, baking, watching movies or spending time in nature.

Printed at Repro India Ltd.